SCAN ME

JIM PEERA

ISBN: 978-1-7375950-8-3

Printed in the United States of America

This book was written in its entirety by real human intelligence.

Front Cover: Selfie by Jim Peera

Dedicated to my human friends
who value, appreciate and celebrate creative
emotional content generated by the beauty of
IMPERFECT and REAL
human intelligence!

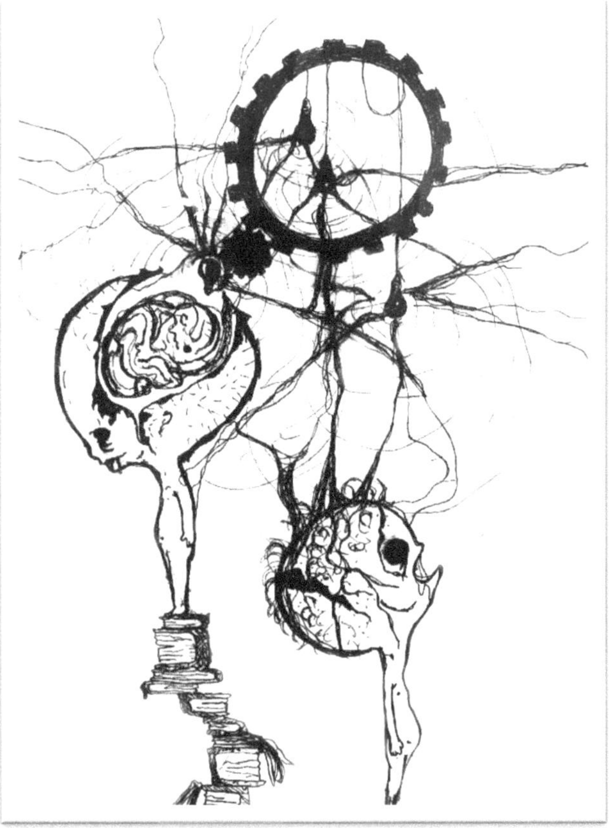

Media: Pen on Paper **Artist: Haseena Peera**

Table of Contents

Human intelligence is not about the intellect, or the mind.

When you stop thinking about this mindfuck,

you will understand.

- Jim Peera

Prologue

There doesn't seem to be the perfect word in any English dictionary to describe a human emotion that excites the body's pleasure, creative, and humor receptors while simultaneously stimulating the intellectual mind; aka being intelligently delicious.

So, I decided to create that word: *INTELICIOUS!*

The poems in this book are therefore written to provide you with not just a dopamine high, but to release a cacophony of neurochemicals to jolt the conforming and programmed brain you've been carrying your entire adulthood – and unfuck it!

As a surrealist, I often use metaphors, double entendre, and humor to explore human behavior without reservations. This gives me the freedom to create and execute creativity for *my* pleasure – in order to give *you* the most authentic experience. Hence, this book is not for the conventional and closed-minded and may provoke, disturb, offend, and discomfort many of you. And that's beautiful because art is our truth mirror and poetry is the language of the soul.

Each poem has been sifted in chronological order for your ultimate experience. Take your time to read, pause, re-read, and fully digest the content of this mind-*pleasuring,* mind-*destroying*, mind-*opening,* mind-*blowing*, mind-*freeing* and.... mind-*fucking* book!

Finally, please become a part of my relentless mission to manifest more love and light into the world - by sharing any poems that moved you with your friends and commenting online and on my websites listed in the back of this book. And don't forget to take a few minutes to leave a review wherever this book is sold.

Thank you!

The Creative Being

A human being's greatest power lies not in the creation of technology, economics, religion, politics, education or other competitive models, but in the untethered rebellion of rebalancing those systems using its innate artistic creativity, imagination, and individuality, that can only be activated by deactivating all man-made attachments to fear, ego, greed, judgment, and mob mentality.

Photo by Jim Peera

Bestseller

Tell me author and wannabe writer, don't you write to get published
valued, read, and to be a famous storyteller
I mean who doesn't want to get lucky by getting big fat checks
and be labeled a bestseller

Especially in America, where you'll get there by entertaining people
with catchy one-liners and fancy packaging, just to get you accolades
Mind you, you don't have to be creative, or thought-provoking
but shallow enough to get you popularity 'Likes' in spades

You'll want people to agree with you without any controversial
or un-sanitized subject matter and get them lazily comfortable
So, their hearts won't skip, bleed, or burn up reading any material
that's too deep, real, or smart to make them uncomfortable

You must be careful not to insult any type of people, especially
the blindfolded, easily-offended, or the pacified crowd
These souls have been starved from humor and imagination for a while
now sleepwalking and mummified in their robotic shroud

You must also know that you'll always get back word for word
what you put out into the technocratic Western society
Maybe your book can be titled 'Humans in The Age of Mediocrity'
or does that dose of truth make it seem like an impropriety

But seriously, I know how hard it must be as a writer these days
to sell yourself like a street prostitute just to be validated
Thank God you got that AI pimp ghosting your book that will now
become so perfectly artificially-inseminated

And the shittier your shit, in a rigged game of assembly-line printers
publishers and marketers, the less you'll have to pay-to-play
They've all sold you out to the fat-cats and hungry vultures' game of
dumbing-down, and profiting off the red, white, blue sheeple's decay

Welcome to a new chapter in human devolution, where from sea to
shining sea, folks have normalized the attention spans of goldfish
with mindless creators pushing buttons to spit out eye-candy content
to serve their fickle fans, another brainless literary drug-dish

Lucky for me, I don't write to be a bestseller, or to appear popular
trying to kiss anyone's ass to be valued, published or even read
I write for the benefit of me, and the rare humans who want
their minds freed, hearts ignited, and souls authentically fed!

A Better God

And then Man

Who had out-Sourced

All of himself to an invisible entity

That kept him forever frustrated

And to the spying machines

That were created to defraud

Eventually realized a smarter

Way to connect to his Source

That was now visible, accessible

Accountable, and non-fungible

By hooking up with

A better God....

SCAN ME

An Exclusive YouTube Video!

Eyes

So
What does
That jackass
Have in him I don't
To deserve that hot girl
Asks a sadfuck white man in his
Jealous voice
Pudgy face
Pouty lips
Hairy ears
Dirty hands
Pointy nose
Stocky body
Jelly potbelly
And flabby ass.

Photo by Ralph Williams

Size

From north to south
It boasts its immense size
Yet, through God's eyes
It's just a droplet in the skies

But it knows the cargo it carries
Depends on it, rain or shine
From microbes to mountains
Its job is never on any to confine

By not containing its vast seas
It opens you beyond what you can see
Giving us blind humans a clue
To set our limitations free

From head to foot
Why must we measure a smaller man
Sizing him up to be less than he can be
Like a big fish stuck in a little can

Or can we dismantle our mind's borders
To accept a sea of Man, so unbound
Mimicking the earth and its oceans
And let him sail infinitely abound!

Natural Wonder

Hello my beauty, a yin yang partner of calm and chaos
and God's wondrous creation
You are like the leaves, branches, and roots to sustain my life
and bring me sacred sensation

You don't always have my back as you often sway with the wind
from one place to another
It must be the leaf personality in you that's restless and curious
to float onto others and to newly discover

You're also quite fragile and break easily with any type of storm
or heavy winds around you
It must be the branch in you that's grown itself too thin and long
and needs on it a good screw

You are highly resilient, strong, and stay grounded during
red rains and being soaked wet
It must be the roots in you that go deep under and wrap
all around to sustain you, I bet

You have had my undivided attention since my own conception
I'm sure you are aware
It must be your Divine life-giving qualities, and there's no other
on earth like you to compare

You must know that in your dry seasons and the bloody hellish
men-oh-pausing weather
Your existence is the perfection of duality, a mix of ups and downs
that can get hard as a bullet, yet feel soft as a feather

And what a natural wonder you are in your bare Brazilian wild state
to always blow my fucking mind
Wow vagina, thanks for allowing me to savor in all your
delights and to enter your sacred door to mankind!

Photo by Donna Peera

Naked

You were born naked weren't you human
and no one ever looked at you as being weak
to be in contempt, have shame, or be a disgrace

So why are you now in your grownup body
having an unnatural habit of covering up your skin
from head to toes, and even masking your face

Was it religion, politics, or the fashion police
that mummified you and profited from always
wearing in public a condom made from loom

I don't recall you or your mother getting cited
and fined for unlawful indecent exposure
as you busted out from her bare womb

Unless of course she lived in a society
where people stopped fighting to be free
and retreated like sheeple, in their glass tomb.

In My Way

Yesterday
I did not ask for me
To be here
But today
I am here
And made in some
Mysterious way.

Today
I will not ask for a tomorrow
Because tomorrow
Is now-here
And the rest
Is all in
God's say.

But every day
I must ask why
The hell I put
My mystery, my God
My yesterday and my tomorrow
In my life's way, anyway?

Health Nut

Look at me world, can't you see how well-balanced I am in my health plan
getting my daily workouts at the gym unlike the average unhealthy man
Look at me world, pushing those heavy barbells up and down my pelvis
while giving my crotch and back the pain they deserve for being so stiff
Look at me world, spinning on the bike and working my weak knees off
while keeping myself hydrated with fluorescent liquids
Look at me world, as my heart pumps on that fancy treadmill
while listening to fake news dumping white noise in my head
Look at me world, sitting in the sauna draining my body of toxins
while angry rap music blasts through my killer EMF headphones
Look at me world, as I get on my wobbly knees to do girly pushups
while texting my flabby ass to nobody about nothing that really matters
Look at me world, as I lift weights to show off my steroidal biceps
while hoping to ride an online girl on my potbelly tonight
Look at me world, as I take myself to the hardcore limit
while I multitask on irradiated devices, being already mentally unfit
Look at me world, wearing swanky sneakers doing the Staying Alive strut
while you get so jealous of this badass American health nut!

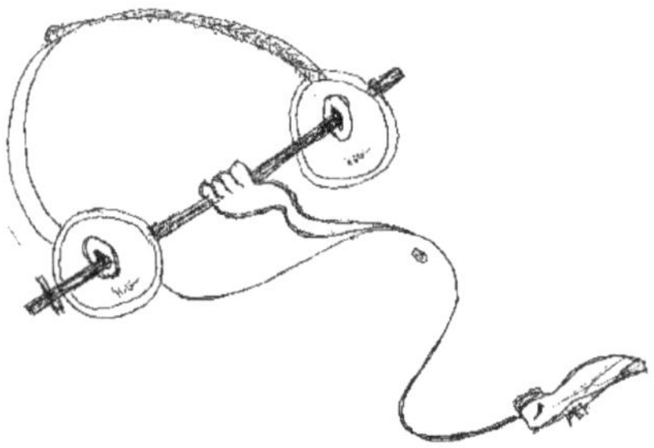

Art by Jim Peera

Lost Without You

There's this unreal feeling I can't explain
A sense of loss fills my emotions so frantic
Searching relentlessly to caress you
And fondle your sexy hard body, once again
Unknowing in my heart how our relationship
Made so habitual could turn this romantic
As I am in the dark and lost without you
Like a wandering cocaine addict
Unable to find any peace in my brain

Not sure why I must have you all to myself
Perhaps it's because you provide for free
All the smart answers I need
Or is it that the questions I have
Overload my mind to easily bleed
For sure, I hate you when you talk crap to me
When I'm on the toilet or smoking weed
Feeding me so much shit at times
To want to tell you to go flush yourself

Maybe I'm codependent on you and such
My doctor and my therapist even tell me
That I masturbate way too much on porn
Having a bad habit of a lonely sex-throb
Holding a loaded gun too hot to touch
Never refusing a trusty hand job
To ease the pain of this human so torn
Who's afraid to set himself free
Or to see our bond as too much

Many are gossiping about us at church
As if it's a lost-lover's curse
That's turning into a Christ-like crutch
But then look who's talking
The religious who are in bondage with you
Are also stuck on you like crazy glue
Jesus, aren't they but hypocrites
If they see our love for each other
To be more than a passionate urge

So, where the hell are you my blessing
And digital dopamine drug
That I can't seem to ever unhook
It seems like hours since I lost you
A bad addiction I just can't shrug
Now, please show yourself to me fast
Before I awake from my dreamy napping
And start reading this here sexy book
To make me feel alive and less depressing!

The Next World

Prepare yourselves, earthlings of sound-mind

Dismantle all your weapons of mass indoctrination

Adapt to the exciting next world of decentralization

Act now, or forever *you* will stay enslaved behind!

Anusthesia

How do you expect me to not feel any pain, suffering, injustice
and inhumanity, alas
When I'm just awakening from the anesthesia you've been pumping
up my privy white ass

The life of comforts you've provided me, waving your flag and praising
your trusty God is painful
I must thank my open mouth for having the courage to say
I'm now more shameful than grateful

The image of greatness you flaunt of me by saying we're the trusty
good guys, is my suffering
I must thank my open eyes for having the foresight to look deeper
and peel off this false covering

The outcries of the powerless victims that you've hidden from me
is exposing your injustice
I must thank my open ears for having the curiosity to listen to
the real orchestrators of justice

The moral fabric that you've tried so hard to tear and rip from me
is unravelling your inhumanity
I must thank my open nose for having the sense to know not to
desensitize your stench of genocidal insanity

The truth is that my mind and body having being comfortably asleep
by your lies is yesterday's news
Today is my day to wake up and ask why I should enjoy murdering reds
browns, blacks, yellows, or even jews

Yes, I must thank myself to have finally decolonized and purged
my pure-blooded Caucasian self from you
For every missile that kills a Palestinian child, shoots through my heart
to numb it, as it bleeds my brain red, white and blue.

Selfie by Jim Peera

Busy Bees

What has happened to us human busy bees, tell me please
Has life's honey become so bitter to eat and provide a healthy fun release

From popular dance nightclubs to live bars and restaurants
You'll get more talk and show than any real tail to satisfy your wants

A pretty girl is all dressed up in pink and white lace so see through
Yet, she's got no interest in shaking her peaches for a joy ride with you

A handsome guy flaunts his ripped body and has his muscle shirt on
Don't get too excited, his banana is too soft for your wet pussy to hang on

She has the moves to tease men and keep their hungry ego on steroids
He has the balls to play with single lonely women like they're humanoids

Both will be pre-occupied though, comparing each other's fake selfie
It's a new human distraction to make them appear all excited and sexy

So, my friend you might as well get drunk and be stupidly high
Now's a good time to numb yourself below the waist and tell the mind a lie

Because no hottie's opening their beehive and sharing any honey tonight
We've stopped enjoying another person's real flesh and sweet delight

Welcome to a new world of sex naysayers, instead of active pollinators
Yes, the busy bee humans are turning into abstainers and masturbators!

That Sweet Date

Like the fresh fruit growing on a tree of sweet delight
Never take for granted your first innocent touch
With its young skin so fragrant, soft, and tight
And everything about it just right, but not too much

For if you brought that date home to gracefully age
Seldom will you get excited to eat it all the time
Having it gotten dry, hard and wrinkled inside a cage
Wishing it had stayed for you, forever sublime.

Exponential Growth

What if there exist many Gods whose only purpose is to be entertained by
our crazy actions
Would Man satisfy them, or just piss them off by being too busy with his
wasteful distractions

We know the Gods are probably belly laughing seeing Man sabotage his
own species
As Man keeps walking, talking, and spitting out from his mouth a crapload
of toxic feces

Looking down at the Man-made version of our creation, these Gods surely
roll their eyes in glee
But alas, it's Man's eye-for-an-eye battle with himself that makes him half-
blind and unfree

As the Gods stomp up and down on their feet in frustration to get Man's
undivided attention
They discover how it's Man's uprooted soul that corrupts his mind with
divisive ill-intention

With time running out for Man, the Gods raise their hands in indignation

to bring out the sun

It's Man's last chance to awaken from his darkness and amuse them

with some real acts of fun

Being patient with their flawed creation, the Gods' only demand is for Man

to make them smile

Unsure how to please his Creators, Man gets nervous and
relieves his fears

by urinating on a baby cactus, doggystyle

Although the Gods are not humored by Man's dumb ways to shrink

and destroy himself existentially

They sure laugh their assess off by his ingenious ways to fertilize

And help grow nature exponentially!

Photo by
Donna Peera

If it is to be

It's a magical day on planet earth, and I'm having an amazing
time escaping away
Never have I felt such heart pounding experience on this
picture-perfect breakaway

Standing atop China's most majestic mountain and looking
five thousand feet down below
How will I forget this birthday trip to the sacred Mount Taishan
appearing in its reverent glow

Its six thousand-steps to the summit seem too cool to climb
and brag to my friends about
But how can I pass up the cable car ride and marvel at the
picturesque vistas to tout

Imagining a soaring eagle's vantage from where I am
is even more breathtaking than scary
I see the graveyards of emperors that once worshipped here
making it all appear so extraordinary

As I swivel around a hundred and eighty degrees, there's nothing
in my view I cannot explore
More colorful temples where animal sacrifices were performed
and Confucius came to mentor

The locals swear to sensing ghosts everywhere that tease the living
on any foggy day
It has to do with connecting with our human spirit energies
but I don't feel anything today

Wise words etched on ancient stone tablets confirm how Buddhism
and Taoism started here
I see thousands of years of man's history right at my fingertips
How, it all seems distant but so near

Wonder if Lao Tsu wrote any of the eighty-one verses of the Tao
Te Ching on this mountain
My imagination is running wild and inspires me to look at life
not as a drain, but as a fountain

It's time to make my way down now from this Jade Emperor Peak
to the village base
These eyes, hands, and brain need a good rest and I must wipe a tear
off my pale face

Wow, what a magnificent joyride I've had today with so many

cool life lessons in philosophy

Especially, when this adventure was all possible by wearing

my fun goggles of virtual reality

But for today to be really epic, I must experience this mountain in person

and set myself free

By getting off my ass and practicing the ancient sages' wisdom of

'If it is to be, it is up to me!'

Stopped

I stopped waiting and waiting, didn't you

For the world to become good, beautiful and kind

When I realized at my birth why I cried

As it was already cut in half by the sharp knife

Of the unhealed human who was looking at me

With worms feasting over the ugly mind.

That Voice

Shh! can you just be quiet for a second and listen to that
soothing voice in your head
It's not the one that makes you afraid of the void
but that other sacred one instead
You may not know why you miss it, but it resonates
like the cry of a dove
Which is why it's best to cancel all noises that
don't serve you any love

You can start by listening to that voice inside
about who you are truly
A human who is fast becoming a slave to
artificial machines so unruly
Or is it that you hate the sound of your own
company so much
Which is why you're constantly wearing earphones
headgear and such

You might do well by trusting in your gut instinct
a little more

It has a way of guiding you to your intended
destination for sure
But then again, you'll doubt yourself for not using
your newest smart devices
Which is why you're stuck relying on all things
of high-status prices

Sometimes it's best to surrender to a part of you that
knows nothing
Having such innocent ignorance, removes all pressure
to be anything
Yet, you may often feel lonely and be unable to carry on
with your day
Which is why you fall on deaf ears by social media
hoping to run away

All these distractions have surely cluttered your mind's
restless hard drive
Only to drown that one absence of audibility within you
that makes your inner music come alive
No, you're not Mozart, but you are smart enough to disconnect from
most outside noise
Because it's in the sound of silence that you'll find peace and
hear your own God's voice!

My Lonely Friend

I don't have many friends, but if I did, they'd probably be
a reflection of me
And since I feel comfortable in this earthly cage, I'd attract someone
who is also not free

What I'd be OK to have is a friend who's a little smarter than me
but not too clever
In that way I won't be jealous, but I'll get my basic needs met
and shit on them never

When they call me, I want to make sure I always answer promptly
and am all ears
It's amazing how much love pours out from folks after emptying
a few cold beers

Whether these friends are socialites or introverts won't matter to me
much anyhow
As long as they keep their bottles of lotions near their beds and
don't ask me to bow

Optimally, I'd like a friend who can speak the same language as me

as to best dialogue

If not, who knows what type of confusion we may get into barbequing

an actual hot dog

Wait a minute, thinking about it aren't you that person who fits the

image of this friend

You think I'm your best friend, but you're that sadfuck human

I have a right to offend

Yeah dude, I'm your obedient dog that you've imprisoned to cover up

your lonely ass

Now, do me a favor and set me free, by adopting a mirror of yourself

... a pet jackass!

"Honey, I got your dog on the grill!"

Why Do I

not shed parts of myself
like a tree that releases
its leaves in the fall,
to let go of the beauty
that once was, but
is now dead weight
and no longer serves
it's natural state at all

Why do I choose to cling
stubbornly to all parts
of me that are ugly
dying and long dead
that stunt my growth
and uproot me
to reap the seeds
of my unnatural downfall?

Whitever

You've got eyes wide open but you're so comfortably blind
My skin's got you uncomfortable in your closed mind

Your blushed face musters a smile but it's forced and fake
An ancestral mask you wear to hide the resentment and hate

That nose you carry up in the air looks so privy and funny
It knows how to detect the smell of my hard-earned money

The ears on you are sharp like a barn owl hunting for its prey
Seems like eavesdropping on me is your idea of power play

Those tightly clenched fists that seem always ready to battle
They're only protecting your false fears you need to grapple

That restless brain that fights all day to be at peace and silent
It works hard to justify your need to provoke and be with me violent

Your mouth that loves to spew anything and everything so negative
If it swallowed its pride, it wouldn't be so ignorant and insensitive

Looking at your body language, it talks with an accent of confusion
Torn between the heart and the soul that don't work in exclusion

Whether you're aware or not, this need to control and occupy my space
Reveals the regretful actions of your people's history you cannot erase

But that was yesterday, and all that matters is what we must do today
For what I'm about to propose makes total sense, unless you're gay

All our beautiful pigments in shades of black, brown, yellow or whitever
Are but an ugly excuse about being pure, special, superior, and whatever

Because when we remove the blinders off our eyes filled with lies and tricks
It is then, we will awaken and see how it's in the mix that racism starts its fix

So, I say why miss an opportunity to stop using our skin as a human dagger
And start procreating like rabbits with each other, so race will no longer matter!

White Powder

Thank you, British colonialists for your history of ugly disgraces
Brainwashing generations of dark-skinned humans in the world
To see themselves as inferior and subservient to Caucasian people
And then selling them toxic white talcum powder to pretty their faces.

Uncork My Universe

The night will be sexy under the stars, planets, and a moonlit sky
They'll all dance for us inside this fine bottle of wine as we get high

It's an old vintage from an uninhabited island in Greece to the south
The Gods have promised that it will be like a party in the mouth

Just one sip of this elixir gets you hooked in a web of delight
For sure, I must save its cork and stow it in a special place tonight

Many around don't approve of us emptying the mind and letting go
They sit and judge in jealousy, while we savor in its delight real slow

The doctor says it's just a weary brain that we're suffocating
Hey doc, I see it as a mind-vacation, being how it's always overstimulating

The yogi pontificates that we're numbing our body's faculties
OK wise guy, I respect the wisdom, but trust in the universal truth of dualities

The shrink thinks it's just another crutch to mask our unhealed self
Got it brainiac, but what if you first fix *your* own mind and lighten up yourself

The astronomer reveals that the stars we are seeing are not really there

Yes star-child, now can *you* come down to earth and get twerked by a sexy derriere

Because I'd rather be high on life dancing myself to some sensual excitation

Then be wasting every drop of this expensive Dionysus's yummy libation

Now tomorrow you can be my doctor, yogi, shrink, or astronomer for me to justify

But tonight, be my cork and I'll be your corkscrew to pop the universe wide open

and dance in your mouth to satisfy!

Media: Mixed on amethyst. Artist: Jim Peera

Shuck Me

It's considered to be a natural medicine for soothing the mind, especially

when eaten in its raw state

Being so unusually delicious, its sweet elixir lingers for days in the
mouth's palette to salivate

Scientifically proven to be an aphrodisiac for earthlings of all sexes

it teases all our five senses

Not sure exactly what chemical it releases, but it quickly calms the nerves

and hostile offenses

Typically, when it's in a closed position it behaves unruly, erratically, and

even irrationally

To assuage this condition, studies have shown great results if it's handled

more gently

Many admirers try way too hard to only get hurt and even bleed trying to

forcefully pry it open

Often, it's an inability to contain their excitement as it tastes like succulent

sushi fresh from the ocean

Once successful though, this extraordinary delicacy of life always satisfies and heals in a lickety-split

Its plump and juicy meat emits a sea-breeze fragrance unlike any other for us humans to easily submit

Yes, this wet pink oyster is definitely a pearl of the Gods to always harvest and carefully shuck

Just ask any man or a lesbian about the health benefits of the incredible-edible vagina to love, savor and suck!

Assage

Hmm, not sure about all you

fat-bottomed people

butt this little

flat-assed human

could sure use

a good assage

right now!

Eyeful

It's not that you're an ordinary un-present ditz
Sitting by my jet-strapped ass for hours in its wits

And are fixated on multiple screen splits
While you feast on your digital porn grits

It's just that I'm looking beyond where you sits
Getting an eyeful of God's wondrous gifts

And it's not *your* mountains that give me the hard-on fits
But these other two extraordinary sexy white tits!

Photo by Jim Peera

My Life Train

I am a teacher and a student for life trying to be a fountain for you
not a drain
If you want to drink from my cup, how about emptying yours before
you ride on my life train

A cup that's already filled, risks spilling its contents where
it's not needed
Whereas an empty cup is always ready and eager to be filled
when it's depleted

It's going to be quite a trip up the mountains, down valleys
and around sharp curves
What you fill your cup with, will determine what happens to
your anxious nerves

First, let's fill it with wisdom that says the journey is more important
than the destination
With these wise words, you will be on track to live each day
with more joy and excitation

Second, you must be curious to explore and try out all types

of new adventures

It's in the richness of life experiences that the Spirit in you shines

to reveal its treasures

Third, you must have focus and stay on your chosen path

traveling everywhere

The modern life of too many choices and distractions

will take you nowhere

Fourth, you must be fearless in taking action and making

important decisions

This one-way train ticket you bought is non-refundable

with no special provisions

Now that you've filled your cup with some important life lessons

for the day

Do you mind if I empty mine too, before I start this train and

we get going today?

Art by Jim Peera

Remove Thy Stick

Thou must know thyself

From the way thou

Walks, talks and acts

That thou art

A pain in the ass

And a royal dick

Yet, who better than thee

To sit still alone naked

For one minute

In front of

A truth mirror

And remove thy stick?

Media:

Clay on

Amethyst

Artist:

Jim Peera

Unholey

Hey human
I see you love to get yourself
Into all sorts of holes

And not just the ones
That make happy
A hard stick and lonely balls

But those that make
Your dumbass to get in easy
And the getting out, a real bitch

The ones you help dig and keep open
To slowly bury your own soul
In a deep dark polarized ditch.

Art by Jim Peera

Y'all Stuck it To Me

You know why I cried when I got out, don't you
Y'all stuck it to me quite bad, being I was half blind
Not knowing what was a lie and what was true

Y'all played me as a fool in your self-righteous Godly ways
Dressing me up in fancy grownup clothes every Sunday
That you worked your ass-off to pay for on Mondays

Y'all thought you taught me what was right from wrong
Walking me to a building lined with yellow prisoner buses
That had me tied down with shiny caution-tape all yearlong

Y'all told me to work hard and pay my dues in society
Being loyal and indentured to the masters of war and slavery
That trained me how to handle money with impropriety

Y'all showed me how to go for the kill in the rigged game of life
Losing competitions while bringing home awards and trophies
That sat beside my trusty bottles of pills and a butcher's knife

Y'all had my life already planned for me, remember
My dreams, ambitions and even my wildest fantasies
That have yet to manifest, unless I stop being a pretender

Hey mom, I was already Spirit-dead getting out of your womb
Stuck with y'all's earthly labels, and false identities suffocating me
As I now lay buried alive, staring at the open door in this glass tomb.

In Light of Evil

Stop pointing to dark forces
As the cause of our evildoing
and the heart's upheaval

It's the absence of the light within
that has blinded our eyes
to not undo the mind's evil.

A Matter of Energy

We're all made up of energy you and I, like the stars that live and die
The big difference is that we're a solid physical matter that we occupy

Our flaws are inherent from the time we enter this earthly atmosphere
Often ignoring nature that shows us better ways to live in this biosphere

But our arrogance has duped us to believe we're the superior species
Polluting ourselves from the inside out, and unable to stand our own feces

It's not enough that we destroy our habitat with toxic chemicals and waste
We've got to fuck with each other, turn ugly, and be two faced

As the darkness unleashes onto us from sundown to sundown
Our candle light is extinguished by sadfucks wearing their masks of frown

Bitchy attitudes of negativity stick to us like lumps of crazy glue
Gnawing their way into the flesh, poisoning every cell in me and you

How do we heal the stress and hurt without painful stitches
Don't worry, I have a solution for not getting inside those ditches

Why bother carrying a burden of a physical body with a heart and mind
To be used, abused, and thrown in a dark hole of the lost and find

I'll just visualize myself as a fearless higher vibration energy field
Like the cosmos that protects itself in its gaseous shield

By seeing myself as a formless energy ball, I'm now unfuckable
Unlike the earthly version that's fragile, and easily fuckable

Mine has no organs like the heart to break or the brain to defecate
It's un-penetrable, feels nothing, cannot think, or even self-mutilate

It's invisible, limitless, boundless, and more powerful in every way
Ready to take on any lip service and not fall into anyone's doomsday

At its worst, it turns me into a supernova, filled with bright radiant gas
So whatever shit humans throw my way, I'll just blow it all outta my ass!

Art by Jim Peera

Zero Sum Game

I am the earth, the moon, the sun, and the spinning balls of fire in the
Creator's universe
My purpose is to keep you in Divine light and shape you up for the better
not for worse

I am the win-win, the yin yang, the paradox, and the mindbender in your
matrix reality
I help you create something from nothing, unless the robots have already
turned you into a nobody

I am the journey from nowhere to everywhere, making your head turn
round and round
My presence has no beginning or end, unless it's the busy mind that
buries you underground

I am the wheels that turn forward on your earthly path and take you to your
destination of bliss
Being always in motion I'll get you there, unless it's the holed-heart that
stops you trying to get a long-due kiss

I am the eyeballs that see through the truth mirror of consciousness
in-focus to set you free
Everything will now come to light for you, unless it's the dark spirit that has
you blindfolded, rope-tied and unfree

I am the zilch, the nada, the you-got-nothing, but it's everything, when we
come together number
You know I add a lot of value to your life, unless it's the divided soul that
has you gone asunder

I am oneness, timelessness, inclusiveness, totality, eternity, and the sign
of your Divinity
My warranty is unlimited, unless you're too afraid to ride on my
merry-go-round of infinity

I am the beginning and the end on your roulette of life, that plays
a silly mind-game
My wheel excites to make you anxious, only to take you back to the start
from where you came

I am the one that tests your honesty, morality, ego, greed, and all your flaws
in low vibration
You turn me into a vicious cycle, as you pass the buck around and create
for everyone high inflation

I am the circle of life, the lifecycle, the fruits, the flowers, the balls you need
and the cosmos geometric shape
So do me a favor human, and don't try cutting into my sacred boundary
to separate or to reshape

How about you stop being crooked, sharp-edged, fragmented
and so lame
And be that fully-rounded species in unity, with no time to play life's
win-lose, zero-sum game!

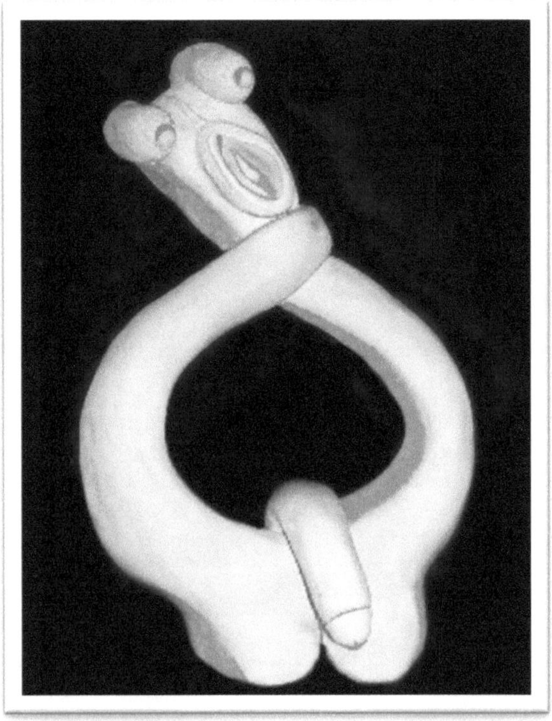

Media: Clay Artist: Jim Peera

Not Alone

Speak as you wish
So, I can trust you
And make this
Loan transaction
Fair and
Bilateral

Do as you must
And convince me
That your word
Will be
My only
Collateral

Act as if you are me
And I am you
So, if you screw me
You know
It won't be
Unilateral.

Time

The greatest crime

You commit each day

Is not knowing that

The meaning of life

Is not wasting your time

Finding any meaning to it

But by meaning to

Live each day like

There is no time.

Photo by Jim Peera

The Spectator

I see you through my glassy eyes that are hypnotized in rear view
Wishing I could do what you do, even if it's only half as well
Yet, I know it's way less work and quicker to be entertained by you
Sipping my morning cup of coffee I didn't even have to brew

Maybe I'm unaware of how blessed I am to live in these push-button times
Sitting on my lazy ass and watching the machines do all the work
Staring you through a camera lens, admiring a fully-activated human
While discreetly recording your performance not seeing the obvious signs

And for whom am I taping this video is a head-pounding question
Is it for a ball-scratching gamer or a finger-trolling sociopath
Maybe it's for the anxious goldfish that swim for my divided attention
Needing more eye-candy to justify their bubble-wrapped domestication

Just yesterday I was awake oozing with passion, free-spirit and high-energy
I created things out of nothing, and had little time to get bored or even sleep
But then I closed my eyes, and much had changed in the modern world
Like a dream, everything got displayed for my pleasure inducing my life's lethargy

Once I played sports, but now I get excited about *you* sweating for me on a screen
Whereas I told dirty jokes and made you laugh, now *you* are my sanitized comedy show
Not long ago I was sexy, now I'm just lame masturbating to an image of *your* vain body
Seems like today the fun is all about *you* satisfying my quick fix of dopamine

Not sure what happens tomorrow, but the earth will keep spinning around full steam
Knowing that its power comes from everything it does, not in what it observes
As the universe shows this fool a lesson to be more of an active participant
For an onlooker of life, is but a dying human sleepwalking in someone else's dream!

Room of Love

Shh!
I am your
Sacred space
For you two
To play inside
And make
Burning love

A quiet place
Where walls
Hear only
Sweet nothings
And the
Laughter
Of a dove

Now mute
The machines
And turn off
All circuits
In your
Computer
Above

Tonight is
The night
To light both ends
Of your pleasure candles
And moan aloud
In my room
Of love!

Zoned Out

I'm all grown up but I'm not growing in here, I wonder why
Becoming too afraid to learn the lessons that don't pacify
Living too comfortably and limited in these lazybones
And not manifesting the teachings of my life zones

I know the learning zone sparks my curiosity
It's here that my knowledge burns in flames of generosity
A place where I am able to learn many important skills
From making kitchen meals to serving bedroom thrills

Being in the fear zone is even more nuts
Where most of what I stress about eats my guts
And when it feeds the beast of self-doubt
It starves the heart with love so drowned-out

Then there's the growth zone that leads the way to transform
It guides the lotus out of the mud and to never conform
This is the one that asks me to apply the lessons learned
To be challenged, and to get the stagnant mind churned

Lastly, there's the pacifying comfort zone to look at
How can I not love this one, to justify being lazy, dumb, and fat
Just ask a Westerner whose body is a poisoned all-you-can-eat buffet
Soaked in bubbly embalming fluids eroding his temple in every way

Now that you're aware of the four zones of life my dear
The comfort, the learning, the growth, and the fear
Can you guess which one matters the most
To not revert me to the land of the shrunk and the lost?

Photo by Donna Peera

Endangered Species

Barely thriving inside a swirling ball of brown dirt
and blue waters
is an enigmatic, and predictable mammal unlike any other
on planet earth
endowed with a natural-born prowess of resilience
internal radar, and creativity
that knows how to survive by endangering itself
and others

Its large size is impressive enough to scare any predator
for better or worse
and trying to compare it to other types of similar creatures
or species
is a mystery to great minds and philosophers like Socrates
and scientists like Darwin
who gave up on it before returning to their home of exploding
balls of gas in the universe

For sure, this mammal behaves like a fiery object when attacked
or asked to submit
expanding its angry googly eyes that are always restless
even in deep sleep
overexerting its large brain that acts impulsively
in moments of fear
especially when it barely uses most of it, but thinks
it's hot shit

What's interesting about this species is its sheer obsession
with its external form
especially its skin color and face features that it uses as bait
to justify attacking its enemy
that it creates by trapping it into little boxes when born
and then reshaping its brains
to behave like it sees fit, only to kill it as an adult
if it does not conform

This creature has intrigued many in the undersea and outer space
realm of the seeing and the unseeing
who truly want to help protect its existence before it becomes
an endangered species

for life on earth would be boring without this mammal that loves
to fuck with its own kind and everyone else
including its whale and dolphin counterparts, that know it only as
a crazy ass human-being!

Who Am I

I'm born in this Spirit-made womb
With hands so pink, delicate and warm
That have become rough and soiled
Handling bags of dirty bills of green
Rendering me old, weary and cold

My karma in this man-made tomb
Is to be unable to wash them clean
But to ask the heart bleeding so brown
Why it's pointing a loaded gun to my soul
That's been long dead and sold.

If Only

If only the world showed you a truer picture
Of a man from a long ago who not only
Soaked His lips in wine
But didn't carry a serious face
How would life be?

If only the world revealed to you a truer picture
Of Him hugging with arms open
Dancing on His airy feet
But not having a white face
How would humanity be?

If only the world awakened you with a truer picture
Of a radical hippie who not only
Sang His heart out
But had a laughing face
How would *you,* now be?

Sew You Know

Sew go ahead
keep making dull excuses
for not stitching up
all your wounds
in your life's needlework

For it's your sharp mind
that has cut you up
into pieces and
turned you into a
human patchwork.

Winner

You didn't win the sperm race
to waste your life's energy
on losers who are
aroused by conflict.

How Deep is Your Love

It's not easy to be married in a world
of the narrow and the shallow these days
keeping up with appearances and hiding
beneath a melanoma of love's malaise

That emotional cancer is non-malignant
your brain may naively think
and what this silent killer never reveals
is how the heart is easy to attack and sink

It knows the flowers you buy are pretty
but are too good to be real
as they've been covered with fake agents
to appear unnaturally surreal

The overtime you put at work
brings home overdue sweet money
yet deep down you know it's a bitter price
you'll pay to keep your bittersweet honey

That smiling face on holiday selfies
validates your masked life
if only the world cared to see
the true picture of this husband and wife

Sadly, neither of you has the guts
to speak your minds anymore
he has let his big balls shrivel and
she has turned her little dick into an eyesore

What's nuts is both of you have lost the ability
to look at each other and openly dialogue
the machines and pets have pacified you
like a hibernating groundhog

Not sure when you'll wake the fuck up
hopefully, before the chickens come to roost
but time is running out on your ass
to unfuck your fate, so self-induced

Because a skin-deep marital conversation
is not authentic communication
it's mind masturbation itching the heart
to end your dying love connection.

Insource

I know I am a more powerful being than they're all programming
us to believe
Every cell in me and you, has the innate ability to self-heal and
pain-relieve
Just ask the brain that produces sixty chemicals, why we need
to look elsewhere
Or, is it just easier for us to be dependent on outer forces for
our healthcare
The machines with their man-made commands are not here
to make you well
They're just turning your naïve ass into an unsocial, lonely
and lazy dumbbell
The pill pushing pimps are salivating as you snooze in your
comfortable den
They'd rather have you sick and addicted to fear, than have you
blissed-out with Zen
The sleepwalkers have no clue being blindly pacified on the
misinformation highway
They're too busy getting drugged on wargames of cheap thrills
and moral decay

The order-takers lost their authenticity, spine, and the clarity to think

a long while back

They'll have to pray for a lightning strike, if they want to get back

on their power-track

How is it that our Creator has endowed us with amazing inwardly tools

to fix any crap

Yet, we choose to contract it out to external sources and be caught

in a false-hope mousetrap

From quieting the restless mind, to activating the energy centers

in our body

There's a doctor, a therapist, a yogi, and everything we need to unfuck

ourselves inside everybody

So the robots, capitalists, zombies, and sheeple may disempower us

to outsource

But I'm smart enough to be out of that jail cell, and invite *you* to join me

to insource!

Selfie by
Jim Peera

Deja Vu

Not too far in the future an autopsy will be done on the demise of our species
Trying to make sense how we hid from the sun and became a lost subspecies
The wide-eyed beings of tomorrow won't look at us in curiosity, but in disdain
Without any doubt, they'll be covering up their shame, confusion, and pain

Once their slinky bodies dissect ours, they'll be ashamed to sew us back in place
It won't be our holed heart, but the shrunken brain that will show much disgrace
Having stored millions of impressions, memories, and programmed commands
They will know it got corrupted and damaged being handled by human hands

Their big heads will be confused about our obsession with bots and machines
How we went overboard with them and reduced ourselves to smithereens
By disrespecting a blue planet with man-made excesses, fears, and rules
We disobeyed the laws of nature and became the universe's king of fools

They'll also be meditating in mid-air trying to alleviate their mental pain
Wondering how we humans turned on ourselves and went so insane
Our frozen blanched carcasses may give them a clue to further analyze
Unless they've already studied our ugly ways, and won't need to chastise

Each will be looking in their mirror of truth and seeing a reflection much too scary
Trying to make some sense of our similarities as recorded in the cosmos library
They'll ponder how we evolved from fish into monkeys and to then just disappear
Or did we stupidly devolve and leave our reincarnated karma for them to fear

These skinny aliens with their colossal heads, googly eyes, and skin so pale grey
Won't be prodding into our human freeze-dried bodies in any special way
Because the funny-looking sun-deficient beings are actually us, in future space
Thanks to the 'Stay Your Ass in The Cage' project to save the white human race!

Monster of Dark

I was born this pale-colored savage and a liar
Who made a musket at a campfire to admire
That I pointed to a red man's head to fire

My life got even more colorful as the occupier
When I knew how to make a bomb to cause hellfire
Wrapped around a tricolor flag to fly even higher

Now I'm this great monster of dark you desire
For the chosen and unhealed humans to hire
And the yellow, brown, and black man to expire.

I Don't Buy it

It's easy transacting into your world
of good versus evil
seeing things as black or white
with haves and have-nots
where heaven is in, and hell is out

But it's not so cut and dry
asking me to choose and justify
buying into your model of duality
when this soul lives in Divine unity
and refuses to be a sellout.

Media: Pen on Paper

Artist: Haseena Peera

Maestro of Peace

You think you're a peace virtuoso in your heavenly ways, but hell I know
you're anything but that, honey
Once upon a time I put my faith in you, now I just see you as an orchestrator
of fear and combat, for love of money

Your loud performances that pierced through stained glass windows
always lured me
Until the sounds of my own silence revealed your motives to keep
me powerless and unfree

The pretty statues of your deceased luminaries you idolize had my eyes
blindfolded for a while
Until my inner vision showed me your ugly mirror of separation behind
every sinister smile

Your shiny leaders that pontificated on podiums in fancy suits of charm
even had my undistracted attention
Until my heart doubled its beat listening to their tarnished words coated with
hypocrisy and tension

You had me convinced that I was a lost human having a spiritual experience
on this sinner's plane
Until my mind questioned all your stories of doom, and books of fear
trying to rewire my brain

In all the years of your existence, you've been good at mouthing your crap
for me and my family's sake
Until my tongue untwisted to tell you, you're just a middleman singing
a tune that's all too fake

You've destroyed more lives in the name of an entity you pretend to know
and I was your fool
Until my betrayed soul awakened to give you up for good and get out of
your crowded cesspool

Don't get me wrong, your infectious chants seem to ease my troubles and
soothe some pain
Too bad they fail to sing a chorus of true harmony, and only exist to
monetize and falsely entertain

So, thanks organized religion for playing your concert of chaos, division,
fear, lies, greed, and illusion
But my ticket to paradise is the God within, who is the *real* maestro of peace,
love, and inclusion!

A Deep Dose

The yogis, monks, and mystics have a certain edge over the ordinary human
By finding a way to enter this portal that unlocks our inside lumen

There's this light within each of us that's on, but for many needs assistance
It requires flipping the mind's busy switch off without any resistance

Why be limited by earthly boundaries, I say to the doubters and naysayers
Much adventure and bliss unleashes from our brain by breaching its layers

Like today at the beach, when radiant energy hovered around me in a dance
One minute I felt alone in the dark, in the next I was in a communal trance

How else was I losing my mind so quickly to unknown faculties so invisible
Only to discover no one was keeping time in that realm and making me invincible

Where could I have traveled to dimensions without a beginning or an end
With friendly alien voices whispering in my head for me to let go and transcend

When could I've seen a laser beam exit from the ocean and pierce my heart
That didn't harm or kill me, but cradled me with warm love to never part

What phenomenon has such power to one moment have me walk on air
But then bring me down to earth like a feather, having gone nowhere

Which chemical factory has this ability to produce in me tears of peace unknown
For sure, the enlightened ones have given us clues by being silent and alone

And by confirming that all these visions that filled my morning with illumination
Were only possible by prescribing to myself a deep dose of third eye meditation!

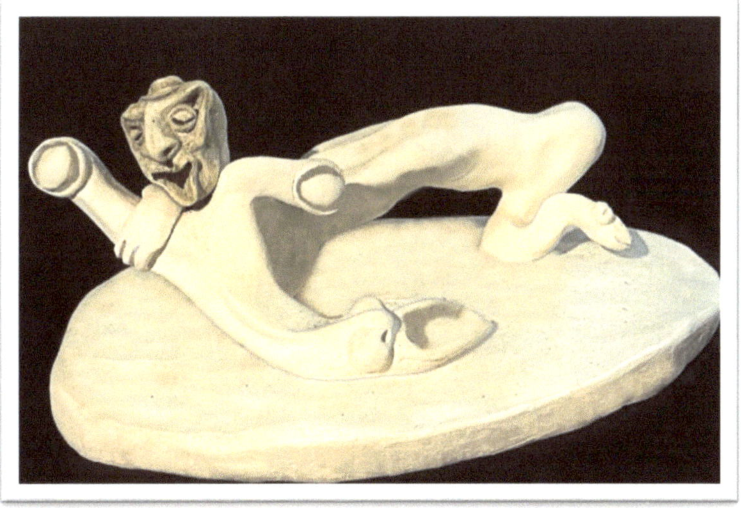

Media: Clay on Clay. Artist: Jim Peera

Sensible Questions

There are so many questions I have for you my loved one
when I see you once again
It's not that I am lost without the answers
but how I keep constantly scratching my head
Staring in the mirror each waking morning comparing the oddities
of women to men
Trying so hard to unfuck the illogical physicality of
our evolved self
Because that MAKES NO SENSE

Why is it that we come from a species with only a nominal
chromosome change
Yet in many ways our animal cousin is so much better than us
from head to toe
With its four legs being more balanced and spine-friendly
for walking long range
Unlike a clumsy human who carries all its bodyweight on its
two tiny feet below
Because that MAKES NO SENSE

Why is it that you made the male body look more like the
wild and hairy monkeys
To want to shave our faces and groom our neanderthal selves
everyday of our life
So that we could not be seen as terrorists, orthodox Jews
or Amish hunkies
Who think they look so cool and sexy, trying to attract
desperate females to take as another wife
Because that MAKES NO SENSE

Why is it that you give the females certain advantages
over the male counterpart
Like its all-you-can-throttle overlubricated engine on high seas
even when it's faking it
While not making any exceptions for horny men with a passionate
and throbbing heart
And not providing them with a quick charger to power up
their love boat's cockpit
Because that MAKES NO SENSE

With such inexplicable differences that you've endowed us with
my Almighty Creator
Here's my first ball-scratching question I must ask you
when I return to see you

Were you playing a joke on us men by putting an unprotected fragile

sac of balls by our ejaculator

Only to be kicked in the nuts by women for acting like animals

hoping to get a good screw?

Because that MAKES PERFECT SENSE!

The Red Door

I am this mysterious room

with walls painted black over white.

Enter through my door

and you'll be stuck in the dark awhile

searching to see the light.

I am this familiar room

with no inside walls, floor, or ceiling.

Enter through my red door

and in no time, you'll be free

having found your place of healing.

Second Brain

I've got this feeling that I'm not as smart as I need to be, you know
An instinctual sensation that comes from my
Belly deep down below

Perhaps I'm neglecting this part of me from sunrise to sunset
An emotional support, trusty guide, and my body's
Most crucial asset

My little brain being its close neighbor only interacts with it in pain
An open relationship that's mutually healthy
For both to sustain

My big brain often talks to it to make me feel good each night and day
An intelligent act to save me from being harmed by
Bad shit in any way

So, I must take care and not hate this thing that sits right atop my butt
An indispensable and smart second brain
Also known as the gut!

Free Medicine

It's seventy-two degrees in Anytown USA, on this pristine sunny day
that I've been gifted
With my ears perked, my nose tickled, my skin delighted
and my eyes uplifted

The wake-up call on my cellphone reminds me to get up
and rush inside my car now
I know listening to loud rap music on my earphones
will make time go faster somehow

The hot coffee in the plastic cup pairs perfectly with jelly donuts
on this morning trip
I know with the windows tightly rolled-up, I will savor them
even more with every sip

The chemical lotions and long sleeves that cover my pale skin
keep me germ-free
I know not exposing my fragile and sensitive-self to fresh air,
dust or pollen is the key

The dark tinted windows keep out the bright sunlight and help hide
my bloodshot eyes
I know staying indoors prevents me from getting melanoma
and is health-wise

The car I drive is like my home and my workplace, that all make me
very comfortable
I know they keep me safe and sanitized, so why should I make my life
uncomfortable

The body that carries me everywhere from day to night is as tough
as I need it to be
I know protecting it from outside intrusive forces is the smartest
choice for me

The brain I wear is sharp enough to not imprison me inside
any type of box or bubble
I know if I don't keep it going with doses of digital dopamine
It will think it's in trouble

Oops, seems like I've wasted an idyllic weather not seeing, smelling
or enjoying this gorgeous earth day
Rushing to my costly allergy doctor I wouldn't need, had I only
prescribed myself some of nature's free medicine today!

Stuck

You've got my brain stuck like a piece of discarded chewing gum
on a cold crowded sidewalk
Feeling used up and stepped on by the weight of the world
hiding its own mental roadblock

Where this brain once had the clarity of a clear sunlit day
now it's grey and heavily clouded
The storms it keeps anticipating have overblown its circuits
readying for it to be shrouded

Where this brain once had the imagination beyond the burning stars
now it's just lame
The artist within seems to have extinguished all creativity
not knowing how it lost its flame

Where this brain once had the resiliency of a bungee cord
now it's stiff and snaps readily
The strength it had to protect itself has been weakened
making it behave unsteadily

Where this brain once had the pleasantry of a wild wallaby

now it's grumpy and mopey

The joy-filled neurons got attacked and hijacked by

an artificial intelligence monkey

Where this brain once had the balance of yin and yang

now it's bogged in chaos unknown

The mind's peace receptors have been disengaged

like an unstable cyclone

Where this brain once had the spark of a playful child

now it idles in neutral position

The aging microprocessor within has rusted

this adult's ignition

Not sure how my brain got stuck in this mental condition

but it's time to get it flowing free

Unsticking myself from the seduction of bad news overload

That has fear-fucked my reality.

Media:
Pen on Paper

Artist:
Haseena
Peera

Care-Less

My whole life I've been caring and self-less
But now you're teaching me to be selfish and care-less

Your advice is quite a mindfuck for a person like me
To flip and reset my past and present reality

You say why drain yourself for the acceptance of another
You must first fill your own fountain, my life partner

It's important to stay powerful for our own well being
Putting ourselves in first position is not a bad thing

When you're looking out for no one but yourself
You will value and appreciate you, in and of itself

You can't give out what you don't have, they say
Being happy and loving thyself must be our default pathway

Perhaps it's time I start prioritizing myself and to self-care
Or else my life will be lived for others and lead to nowhere

For nothing makes sense and everything makes sense you see
It's the duality of being in balance and setting myself truly free

So, honey, this advice is like the one you gave me on stimulation
Where you told me to go unfuck myself, using masturbation!

Smooth Criminal

If there was a day to celebrate your favorite occasion
what would it be
could it be something that inspires you to feel rich
or to be happy and free
And if you chose to be all that, how would you
spend that day
preferring to be kosher and not partake in anything
you had to pay

I'm not talking about occasions like Hannukah or Eid
but many others
like those that are aimed to fire-up lovers, fathers
and mothers
Not to forget the ones with scary ghouls, dead turkeys
and cute bunnies
that shoot holes in your wallet from bullets made of
shiny plastic monies

These celebrations that hit you like colorful sparks flying on
Fourth of July
are but an excuse to burn your money on Black Friday
and to self-gratify

Maybe it's your idea of keeping up with the Joneses
and looking good
only to realize you've been played like a naïve child
in your not-so-wise adulthood

At some point you'll wake up to the truth
of your material cravings
as they slowly devour what's left of your skeletal
spiritual savings
The elders who are dead gone are surely
laughing in their grave
having lectured you to deaf ears to consume less
and seriously save

Now that you've opened your eyes to the reality of being
robbed blind
and aren't happier or freer by celebrating yourself stupid
into a financial bind
Do you blame the smooth criminals for seducing you to play
a game of win-lose
or do you kick yourself in your dumb ass, for making richer
the elites, the corporations and the Jews?

Disposable

Not too long ago if anything was made anywhere in Asia

it was of poor quality

Being fragile and easily discardable, Asian products held a reputation

of being cheap and shitty

Back then however, most American-made consumables

never really sucked

Today, if you buy any of it, you'll put yourself in more debt and bend down

to be fucked

Back then the Mom and Pop stores sold you those things with integrity

and no lip service

Today, big monopolies shamelessly stick it to you, unless you buy

their fake warranty of disservice

Back then the salespeople were honest in warning you of the dangers

of what you bought

Today, the robots and machines interface with you, so the sleezy rich

earthlings don't get caught

Back then you knew you got what you paid for, especially if it was from

Japan or China

Today, they call it planned obsolescence, so when things die
you won't sue them for getting angina

Back then you got what you were promised by simply shaking
a seller's trusty hands
Today, you'll sign your rights away with slimy waivers and lay down
to be slaughtered like lambs

Back then you didn't have any upgrades or trade-ins to fuss or stress about
with your crap
Today, you'll gladly throw it away for another new piece of shit and have faith
in a spying app

Back then we knew the difference between locally made and imported
because our bar was high
Today, we're normalizing mediocrity and can't even rely on our own kind
to not screw us or lie

How things have changed as poor-quality goods & services, and low standard
humans are now Made in USA
A profit-over-people society creating its own shitty and disposable state
to be flushed away!

You Forgot

You told me yesterday
that the reason for
our suffering
is attachment
and how love is
the lifesaver
to free our hearts
from being capsized
by our fears

But you forgot
to cut the rope
from my dinghy
to your boat
until today
and yet still
expect me
to not drown
in my sea of tears?

Shallow

Hey friend, it's like we've known each other for a long time
but I don't really know you
The hello, how are you, and see you later greetings haven't led us
to any personal breakthrough

I see you at the coffee shop many mornings and you'll pause awhile
from your digital distraction
But the small talk about the latte, the weather, or your new nails
don't ever perk up our interaction

We meet at the gym quite often, and you'll mute your unhealthy earphones
to be kind and courteous
But in the short minutes that you exercise your mouth with me
you seem always too impervious

When we bump into each other walking in the park, you'll even be kind
to shorten your dog's leash
But while our pets bond sniffing each other's butts, you avoid talking to me
about *your* shit to unleash

Whenever you invite me to your family gatherings, you'll be your best self
to make me feel comfortable

But behind the superficial smiles and judgment, you hide behind a mask
that looks sadly uncomfortable

You know that still waters run deep, and glassy lakes reflect
everything in poor detail
But if I'm your friend, why not flow freely in richer encounters with me
like an untethered parasail

It's not like you're empty-headed or have nothing substantive to say
when you see me
But how can you grow as a person, if you're afraid to go deeper and learn
to agree to disagree

Do you ever wonder how much better we'd all be, by not being so shallow
and keep small talking with each other
But then again look at where it's gotten you in your relationship with your
own father and mother!

Media: Pen on paper

Artist: Haseena Peera

The Relative Theory

I'm no Einstein, but there's this theory I have about our thoughts,
actions, reactions and emotions
that will make your head turn like a mad scientist holding on to spinning
hands of a clock tower
It's relatively logical to understand if you're a human going around in circles
and racing for time
as you'll end up exactly where you started after going through all the
unnecessary and crazy motions.

How about all the effort you spent last week finding deals
cutting coupons to save
and trying to get yourself out of the work ditch for a vacation
so well deserved
Only to wake up this morning with a minor stroke that took you
to the emergency room
costing you an arm and a leg without insurance, and having you back
in the slave grave.

How about waking up happy that your dream of being financially free
in the golden years
has finally paid off this week after you made all the right investments
in your life

Only to realize that a new reality just robbed you blind
As the guy you voted in office
just screwed you by doubling your taxes, and leaving you
in a raging nightmare of tears.

How about that Spirit-born child that just came into your life
making you so proud
to be a father and becoming much more than your self-absorbed
material self
Only to be told today that your closest best friend you've known
since childhood
just got killed by a sniper, destroying you from the inside
and screaming out loud.

How about feeling so proud for exercising, eating well, and investing
in your health
making you so enviable to all your circle of friends and
even your doctor
Only to get a call from her today informing you that your
bloodwork shows
a rare incurable form of cancer, begging you to realize how health
always trumps wealth

I'm no scientist, philosopher, or psychotherapist trying to unravel

the complex human brain

that plays with our thoughts, actions, reactions, and emotions

all sorts of mind games

But I just proved a theory to you to help me not stress, be anxious

or get depressed, and to affirmatively say

that everything in life is relative, and knowing this truth now stops me

from going fucking insane!

Mindspin

How do you expect me to be still

in the mind

When I am on a spaceship

that's spinning

one thousand miles per hour?

The Runner

There's no time don't you know, for me to stop
and look at your show
I've seen it all before, and am in a hurry to catch the next
act of tomorrow

It was just last year I passed by your auditorium of
musicians so loud
I didn't hear much, except how you were playing to
an empty crowd

It was only last month I walked accidentally across your room
of dancing girls
I don't recall feeling groovy, but stepping on some loose beads
of shiny plastic pearls

It was only last week I dashed into your office filled with
a paparazzi galore
I didn't sense any excitement, as I was rushing myself
out the door

It was only yesterday that I was flipping through the pages
of your future acts
I didn't care to read about any of them, except for
their ending climax

It was only this morning that you reminded me
of today's show
Now, how many times have I said, I don't have
any time for you, amigo

I'm too busy decorating and resuscitating
the dead memories of yesterday
And preparing for tomorrow's dreams, every anxious
minute, hour and day

So, don't wait for me tonight to enjoy the live music
in the concert halls
For I'm but a runner, who only lives to witness all of life's
last curtain calls.

Art by Jim Peera

Laissez Faire American

I'm a proud almighty laissez faire American
Don't criticize me or I'll have to draw out my weapon

I have a right to do whatever I damn please
Fuck with me and I'll bring you down to your knees

I was raised without getting a spanking
And in school I always managed to get a high ranking

I ain't that clever and am definitely overrated
But thanks to smartphones I'm not so dumb and hated

I like staying depressed and sick in the head
It gets me all the drugs while I'm a walking dead

I am angry and I hate everyone who is not like me
It sure trumps being happy, kind and carefree

I have very little coping or social skills
Not to worry, I have faith in my prescription pills

I don't like to read, write or dialogue with anyone
This ass is glued to the screen and it's my idea of fun

I am fragile, fickle and always offended
It's just me being shallow and emotionally bounded

I am obsessed with myself and love to take selfies
It validates me being a trans and an online striptease

I got skeletons in the closet and traumas unhealed
I prefer to keep them all buried and concealed

I am always anxious with an attention span of a goldfish
Keep entertaining me, as it helps me stay selfish

I'm not interested in doing the work to keep anything intact
It's my disposable society's answer to not face any true fact

I love to eat shit and drive my fat ass everywhere
Say what you want but I am proud of this gross derriere

I am a master of complaints and a servant to my ego beast
Go ahead and emulate me, for I am in balance the least

I am really quick to point fingers at everyone but myself
Even my truth mirror looks great collecting dust on the shelf

So yes, I am this badass laissez faire American y'all
I'll do what I damn please, so keep enabling my downfall!

Media:
Pen on Paper

Artist:
Haseena Peera

Slap Me Stupid

Slap me on the head for the way I turned out

But it's *my* zombie brain that struggles to scream and shout

Slap me on the face for being blindly glued to my phone

But it's *my* glassy *eyes* that will get overblown

Slap me on the wrist for being a functional addict

But it's *my* middle finger that's about to get flipped

Slap me on the butt for always disrespecting you

But it's *my* spoiled ass that never got spanked blue

Slap me for all my terrible habits and making y'all look so bad

But it's *you* who were a hands-off passive Mom and Dad

So, slap you and me stupid from top to bottom everywhere

As I too let *my* kids do whatever, to actively go nowhere.

False Servitude

Would putting my two palms together in praise of you my God
mean that I'm actually falsely separated from you
Because if I was truly connected to you and had faith in your plans
for me, I would not fear or bother you in any way, isn't that true?

Could it also ring true to call out your name with every breath
and not just remember you in times of death, hardship, or suffering
Because as a faithful believer I could not be a self-righteous hypocrite
to engage in any acts of unholy worship, business, or money plundering.

Should it make smarter sense for my mind to not rule the heart
and become its master to keep it afraid, broken, and enslaved
Because the Divine-drum of life should always beat strong
without needing the brain to think, or asking love to be saved.

And so then does a true lover of the all-knowing, and the all-protecting
only open his hands to trust you without doubt and surrender in gratitude
For if I close my palms together and pray to you for anything else, my Lord
doesn't that self-serving act become ungodly and in false servitude?

Overloadeth

When a human readeth too much, it ovethinketh

As it overthinketh, it overquestioneth

As it overquestioneth, it overanalyzeth

As it overanalyzeth, it begins to doubteth

As it doubteth , it starts to feareth

As it feareth, it cannot stop to overfeareth

As it overfeareth it, it stoppeth living

And starteth becoming a lonely sadfuck

Until it waketh up from its earthly grave

Wondering why the fuck it never ever readeath

About the dangers of its brain being overloadeth!

Truth

When you stop living vicariously

through the experiences of others

You'll start experiencing living fearlessly

passionately, and authentically

for yourself.

My Destiny

I'm swirling and kicking hard in here to get out

Preparing to cry when I'm ready to breakout

A lot will be expected of me out there, I know

To be like a Buddha, a Plato or even a Picasso

But what if my life is already pre-determined in here

And it's not me, but *you* who'll end up shedding a tear?

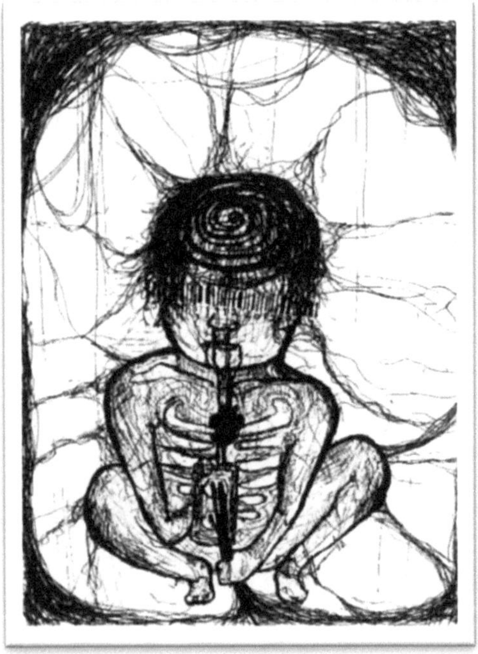

Media:
Pen on
Paper

Artist:
Haseena
Peera

Panopticon

So, I know why

you believe you need to spy on me

but since I know that you're spying on me

and I am showing you what you want to see and hear

it must make you spies want to question

your job of spying on me then

would you agree?

Square

Where are the square eggs my smart humans

with all the geeks and nerds in the world

to engineer another genetic breakthrough?

Perhaps it's the dumbass chickens, they say

who have refused to be put in little boxes

that fit in a perfect world of boring cubicles

to become sharp-edged and uncool like you!

Alienshit

You expect me to believe
That we are so smart
As to fit a whole room
Of computing power
Into a strand of a human hair
In just sixty years.

Yet we can't fix
Our own brain
And stop it
From destroying
Our own species
For thousands of years?

Photo by
Iman Peera

Hot Seller

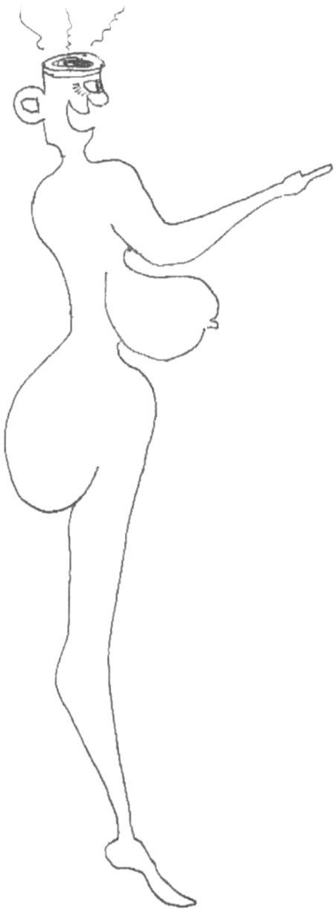

Art by Jim Peera

It's a chilly morning my dear

Time to get our daily fix from

The F-cupped drug dealer

I bet she's ready to serve us

Her hot Italian brain-cheer

The one that she embellishes

With signs of hearts and other

That magically float on foam

With mindfuck messages to

Want to further uncover.....

SCAN ME

A funny short on YouTube!

Monogamey

From dusk to dawn they're both dying from within
He stays alive by overworking and she drowns herself in gin

The life they've seemingly built together for so many years
Has got them sinking in a sea of regret and a boatload of fears

He walks around with his head hanging like a weeping willow
She runs around town flirting with anyone who'll lay by her pillow

One look into each other's eyes and you know they've gone stale
The flame is slowly extinguishing inside their self-induced jail

Their most exciting night out is going to a restaurant to eat
It's where their eyes wander on sexy strangers in discreet

They'll mock, ridicule and judge those they most admire
Don't mind, they're just projecting their longing desire

As the fleeting sun drops off the horizon in a blink of an eye
The man and the woman waste another day waving a sad goodbye

Each will lay side by side tonight like they've done for so long
Both will say they're too tired to fuck and pretend to play along

The full moon looks upon each of them with a crazy gaze
These are the true lunatics who are down there, it says

For sure both of them are good at being poker faced
Wishing their partner for just one starry night could be replaced

Neither has the spine or balls to talk about swinging with some other
They've been programmed by culture and rules to eat no further

That's too bad because even a threesome could reignite their fire
A harmless physical adventure to not feel like a worn-out tire

But the man sneaks out of bed and feasts on an online playmate
As she reaches into her bag of plastic pleasures to masturbate

Yes, they're the sadfuck married couple who play a game of lies
Buying into monogamy and not activating what they fantasize.

Photo by
Jim Peera

Ambrosia

The love Gods refer to it as an elixir behind the third eye
Once excreted, its pleasure takes you beyond any sexual high

There's no wanting or needing anyone's body to be satisfied
This amazing hormonal secretion is the ultimate joyride

When connected to it, you will find self-love and bliss unknown
You'll stop to bitch and moan and forget about ever being blown

Just keep meditating for hours and days without human contact
And this Divine fluid will keep your mind, body and soul intact

Why be so focused on the identity of the physical self they say
Now you'll find pleasure in all people, even ugly and fat everyday

It's known as the ambrosia of life, a beautiful inner ecstasy
Or Amrutha, a Hindu fantasy of immortality

Many East Indians are religiously in hot and anxious pursuit of it
Elevating themselves to a state of pure nirvana to submit

So, this nectar in the pineal gland is well worth experiencing
Too bad that it's against my religion to stop enjoying fucking!

Night Fever

Now tonight my love, let's detox from digital cocaine
Of the cold machines and the stiff robots
By getting out of our heads
Unleashing our free spirit within
Drumming to the beat of our hearts
Dancing to the rhythm of our souls
Making hot love together
And drinking this
Healing elixir
To intoxicate
Our mind
Body
And
Soul
To
The
Music
Of the iconic Bee Gees.

Awe-wakening

I'm sitting here at dusk with an icepack on my balls that have since
this dawn been in pain
Is it a reminder from a higher entity to never forget this day
to have gone so awesomely insane

The distressed heart was pounding from a 4 A.M phone call
screaming for help and urgency
Is it a reminder that I can drive like a maniac doing ninety
for a loved one's life in emergency

The restless mind sped up, down, and around comforting a rabid
human brain out of control
Is it a reminder that I can calm it by cradling a toxified body
on my groin like a stiff jellyroll

The warrior spirit arose to the cries of a capsized vessel held hostage
by an unknown substance
Is it a reminder that my only goal was to bring it back to shore
extolling a sea of patience

This day will be forever embellished in my memory of memories,
even when I'll lose my memory
Is it a reminder that the bites, bruises, screams, and cries of silence
are all etched in the sensory

The heart, mind, spirit, and balls have all suffered today
living in this rollercoaster human reality
Is it a reminder that as an artist/healer I stayed soft, calm
and strong in this mindfuck surreality

The Divine lightworkers are always working mysteriously
to unfuck a seemingly fucked-up day
Is it a reminder that our faith in the light, makes no room for any
darkness in this matrix to stay

And can it be that there are absolutely no coincidences
that get in the way of our Creator's plan
Is it a reminder of appreciating our life's fragility by making
a scary example out of a young man

This is a smart human who educates people on plant-medicines
to help them heal adeptly
Was this his awe-wakening moment to be weary of people
who operate dishonestly and ineptly

If only he knew that I was afraid of losing him to brain damage
and prayed quietly without any rest
Holding him like I'd done when he was a baby helped *me* feel
comforted, protected and blessed

So, thank you angels for saving my son today after he was unduly
poisoned by counterfeit drugs
I'll take the balls of pain, a pounding heart, and a racing mind
in return for his many more hugs!

Scapegoat

It matters not why
your parents
didn't do much
for you when
you were a kid.

But why you
keep using them
as an excuse for
not doing enough
for *your* kids.

Wisdumb

It's having an encounter with a very thrifty

but filthy-wealthy workaholic

eighty-year-old man

who tells you

how he just

escaped

a fatal

stroke

and

how

he had

an epiphany

that having a fun

happy and fulfilled

life in this world is all for

and about the accumulation of money.

Unloaded

You sure bought into my story of loading up and striking it rich, I see
Salivating over my pinnacle of yellow metal so bright and bold
Grinding and hauling your ass up a mountain, so oversold
Knowing your climb to be anxious, lonely and unfree

I sure hope you paused, and not just for gas along the busy road
Feeding all your senses with experiences of shivers and quivers
Uncasing and dipping your tired feet in free-flowing turquoise rivers
Seeing my shiny top only as an illusion, with no gold for you to load.

Photo by Jim Peera

Happiness

Sure, you can complicate it

But I see it simply as;

Having something to do

Having something to look forward to

And having someone to love.

Regrets

Go ahead and kick yourself

For not taking action doing this

Or impulsively doing that

Always looking back, and shaking your head

On your life's couldas, shouldas and wouldas

But you can only have regrettable moments

Never any regrets

Being a flawed species

With an unlimited license to fuck up

So relax, you miserable dumbass!

Embodyment

Each day

Your lips

In the mirror

Yearn for you

To kiss them

Sublime

For never

Do they know

How to kiss

Any other part

Of your body

At any time!

Photo by Jim Peera

Spiritual Selection

The human in us says we're not alone in feeling isolated and alone

It may not be the loneliness, as much as the not-belonging

Not being understood around fake and artificial connections

Where so much of what we need to say, do or create

Gets hijacked today, in a low vibration and selective drop zone

The Spirit in us asks us to ignore all algorithmic social rejection

And to do what a truly awakened soul does to find itself

By retreating into a place of solitude, authenticity and self-reflection

Without avatars, machines, and goldfish-brained humans

To then connect with real people through a higher spiritual selection.

Media: Pen
On Paper

Artist:
Haseena
Peera

Emotion

Two trees

Of lovers in the woods

One born male, the other female

Thought they were both well grounded

Firmly planted down, always looking up

Resilient in chaos, awake in calm

Wise as their ancestors

Having no doubts

Of their gender

Without any desire

To change their sex

Until they heard two

Transgender humans

Making out under them

And laughing their asses off.

Delusion

I know you know what happens
when you don't learn from history
You know I know the ugly reality
of never knowing our real-story

They know we know who they are
in trying to erase and rearrange the past
Wonder if they know there's always karma
in profiting from any type of power-glory.

Up Your G-ass

I'm not trying to be a smart-ass or derogatory
Butt there's a more effective way to get any medicine
Into your body other than through your mouth or the skin
Just smile, relax, bend-over and shoot it up the butt
Straight to your sickly gut, with a fast-acting suppository!

Why

Why bother retiring your trusty old towel
For all the long years you've spent using it
Wiping up all the blood, dirt, sweat, and tears
Have only made it more flexible and stronger
To soak in many more types of liquids
From picking up ice, to putting out fire
And even performing new tricks.

Why Not

Why not learn from the lesson of the useful towel
Showing us how to be unafraid of getting old
Of having many more ways and days still left
To spark our mind, ignite the heart
And light up that immortal soul
As we now look to the golden years
Not as our time to retire, but to refire!

Agoraphobia

Thanks for lecturing me about the comfort zone
That's made me afraid to step out into the open jungle
But I'm not wild about being unsafe and all alone

Thanks for telling me about the super ego too
That's trained my brain from birth to think this way
But trust me I know who I am, I do, I do, I really do

Thanks for warning me of being stuck inside a jail cell
That's held my life hostage in monotony like a machine
But I love it and feel safe in here, so y'all can go to hell!

Media:
Driftwood
And Shells

Artist:
Jim Peera

The Awakening

Someday my friend, you will come to see
As your soul travels to its next destination
leaving your present invisible cage
To reveal that this earthly reality
Was less about the search and find
attachments, winning, or anything else
And more about existing fearlessly
by being truly free.

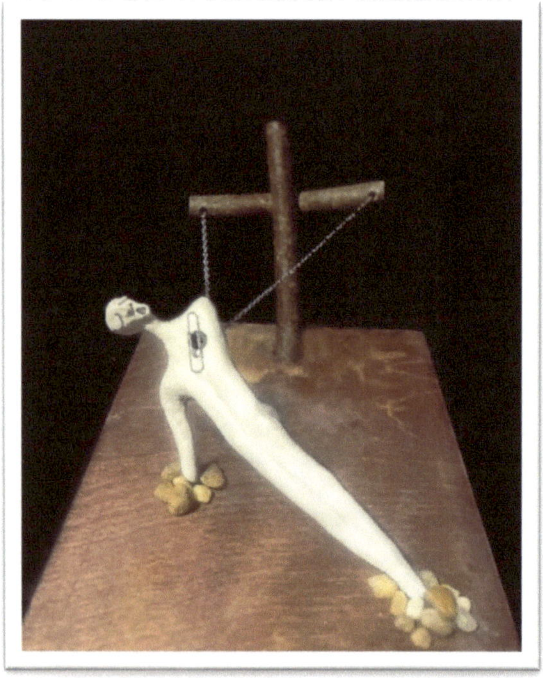

Media:
Clay on
Mixed
Media

Artist:
Jim Peera

Eclips

Why waste your life

Pouting your lips

To the clouds

Of yesterday,

Frowning at the

Storms of tomorrow

And not kissing

The sun of today?

Selfie by Jim Peera

Intelicious

Ask a woman what she wants in a man on a first date, and she'll likely say a good head
Ask that man what *he* wants, and he'll say to have her legs open like a book on his bed

Let's just call it an even-split between having the brains, and the looks to match it too
Or as a renaissance poet would put it, *'Thou shall open thy toolbox to find a good screw'*

For it's no secret that each sex silently reads the others motives, desires, and fantasies
And neither prefers going home a loser, by getting off on cheap porn or dirty magazines

That's because the pleasure receptors within the male and female act the same
To be satisfied, both need a quality mindfucking experience that will not be lame

This is a special time where the journey is often more interesting than the destination

Even if any of them fucks it up, they'll still end up with a good dose of
mind-fornication

To start off, each person will need to make a good impression and
showcase their best self
Working hard on prettying the outer packaging and getting noticed on
love's top shelf

The secret to buying into one another requires ample doses of charm
and humor to impress
These traits will come effortlessly if one knows how to be vulnerable,
let go, and self-express

The Gods of romance will tell them to stay untethered and authentic in
their pursuit to connect
The last thing any new love needs is for the Satan of ego and pretense
to help them disconnect

Taking a closer look inside the cover will take some work, as neither
knows what to expect
The more curious and open-minded each person is, the deeper will be
their trust and respect

If the intention to connect is well-aligned, the results can be highly
cathartic and deeply spiritual

In the worst-case scenario, they'll see it all as an encounter that's
fresh, fun, or even hysterical

Without getting too philosophical, this date will also need to burst
some comfortable bubbles
Afterall, how does any healthy relationship grow by not facing its hard
lessons and troubles

Because isn't this crazy thing called *'love'* always ignited by a
skipping heartbeat for someone
And even when the heart stops beating, the adventure you make
together can never be undone

So, I say why complicate things on your first hot date and just see it all
as intelligently delicious
Like this book you've just read as your new love, now inspiring *you*
to be so fucking intelicious!

Photo by
Donna Peera

You Say

You say not to trust politicians to do what they say
As they lie while smiling and smirking at you all day

You say you're tired of being sold promises by them
As politicians don't deliver on anything, except mayhem

You say you are sick of taking politicians at their word
As their word is as real as a pig flying like a bird

You say you have little faith in a world of sellouts and crooks
As it's filled with politicians dangling on puppetry hooks

You say our thoughts have no value without action
As you actively help politicians paint their art of distraction

You say these politicians are full of shit on the one hand
As you yourself act just like them with your head in the sand

You say you are going to give Jim a review on this book today
Ok, let's see if you truly aren't like a politician, and will do what you say!

And then life got even more intelicious

when

the observer became the observed....

Photo by Jim Peera

Also by Jim Peera…

The Healium Way

'The Art of Being Extraordinary

and Living Without Regrets'

Part 1 & Part 2

Unf*ck

'A Man's Extraordinary

Poetic Journey

Out Of His Life's Storm'

42 Poems

Mindf*ck

'Poetry and Art to

Free The Soul'

63 Poems w/ matching art

Wake The F*ck Up

"It's like if George Carlin

met Dr Seuss at

Animal Farm!"

A children's book for adults

"LIVE intentionally
LAUGH contagiously
LOVE passionately"

- Jim Peera

About the Author

Jim Peera (born Azim Peera), has been called everything from a counterculture renaissance man, to a 'hypstic' (a hippie-mystic).

His life's resume is quite impressive as a non-conformist artist, accomplished entrepreneur, real-estate developer, property rights defender, author, poet, stand-up comic, inventor, world traveler, and warrior of peace.

As a man who dislikes labels or identifying himself with anything, he prefers to be known simply as 'a work-in-progress-human.'

Azim founded the nonprofit interactive wellness-with-the-arts project; Healium Center Foundation in Atlanta, Georgia in 2014. He also self-published a 2-part memoir and self-help book: 'The Healium Way: The art of being extraordinary and living without regrets.' in 2022. In 2023, he published two original poetry books: 'Unf*ck; A man's *extra*ordinary poetic journey out of his life's storm' and 'Mindf?ck; Poetry and art to free the soul.' In 2024 he published 'Wake The F*ck Up'; a satirical children's book for adults. In 2025 he began his smart comedy project 'Unfuck Comic' using standup and video skits to uplift, inspire and enlighten humanity.

Mr. Peera has lived a full and adventurous life and his journey hasn't been short of being *extra*ordinary. Being true to himself, he has always believed in living a life of balance with the medicine of the creative and healing arts as his freedom drug. In addition to his hobbies of sculpting, photography, film-making, sound healing, and drumming; poetry has always been his favorite outlet of self-expression and social commentary.

The multi-dimensional American immigrant from Tanzania, East Africa is a well-rounded spiritual family man with two grown children and a wife of forty-three years. He has lived in France, England, Costa Rica and currently resides in the U.S A.

For more information visit him at:

JimPeera.com

www.ingramcontent.com/pod-product-compliance
Lightning Source LLC
LaVergne TN
LVHW070046070526
838200LV00028B/400
9781737595083